S0-AXZ-415

The

Glorious Church

A Vision of the Local Apostolic Church

Purpose
Headship
Prayer
Spirit and Truth
Ministry
Evangelism
Discipleship
Fellowship
Praise
Endtime Power and Glory
Israel

David Huston and Jim McKinley

www.gloriouschurch.com

The Glorious Church

Copyright © 1999 David Huston and Jim McKinley

ALL RIGHTS RESERVED

No part of this book may be reproduced or transmitted in any
form or by any means, electronic or mechanical, including
photocopying, recording, or by any information storage and
retrieval system, without permission in writing from the publisher
or author; except that permission is granted to reprint all or part
of this document for personal study and research provided that
reprints are not offered for sale.

All Scripture references are from the New King James Version of
the Bible, copyright © 1982 by Thomas Nelson, Inc., Nashville,
TN, unless otherwise indicated. Definitions of Greek and Hebrew
words are taken from *Strong's Exhaustive Concordance* and *Thayer's
Lexicon*.

ISBN 0-9664710-7-5

Published by

Rosh Pinnah
P U B L I C A T I O N S
PO Box 337, Carlisle, PA, 17013-0337
e-mail at RoshPinnah@aol.com
Rosh Pinnah means 'Chief Cornerstone' in Hebrew.

Printed in the United States of America
for worldwide distribution by

Morris Publishing • 3212 East Highway 30 • Kearney, NE 68847
1-800-650-7888

This book is dedicated

to the fulfillment

of God's eternal purpose.

Foreword by Fred Childs

As we enter into the end-time era and begin witnessing the greatest time of harvest in the history of the Church, should we be surprised that the time has arrived for us to examine the structure of the Church? Do our present structures and methods enable us to receive everything God has provided for the building of His house? Are the current popular local church structures even biblical? Are the structures and methods many of us are using derived more from the denominational, secular, and business worlds than from the Word of God?

Mature and honest students of the Word are never offended when an opportunity arises to clarify or verify age-old truths by the Scriptures. But allowing for the sensitive nature of it's subject, perhaps *The Glorious Church* should be read only by those who are willing to examine the leadership and ministerial structures of today's Church by comparing them to the pattern of the first century original. If you have honest questions about these issues, this book offers honest answers.

David Huston and Jim McKinley have studiously and prayerfully prepared a masterpiece of truth and insight. All church leaders who are searching for truth will do well to read, reread, and deeply absorb this book. The authors are not proposing a new and unproven theory; they are simply expounding clear biblical concepts. That they cut against the current grain is neither God's fault nor their's—it is merely a commentary on the present state of our thinking.

I believe this book can open a great and effectual door of revival if the heart and mind of the reader is sincere enough to consider (and eventually accept) its timeless principles. Do we love truth enough to be willing to change anything about our current way of doing things if we are shown by the Scriptures that God has another way? Reading this book could be a first step to answering that question.

Fred Childs, Houston, TX
Leadership Strategies International

Foreword by Dale Rumble

The early Church turned the world of its day upside down. The remarkable thing is that they managed to do it without the organizations, hierarchical control structures, titles, and promotional methods that are so commonly relied upon today. Also, the Bible makes no mention of church buildings such as we have today. What we see instead are the original Christians meeting primarily in private homes.

What was the secret to the exponential growth of the early Church?

David Huston and Jim McKinley have provided clear answers to this question through the use of a creative "contemporary interview" with Paul, the bondservant and apostle of Jesus. Through a series of questions and answers, Paul explains that the Church is not an organization, but rather a Spirit-empowered organism, built to fulfill God's eternal purpose by Jesus Christ, its one and only Head. To Paul, the Church is literally the body of Christ on the earth. How desperately today's Church needs to rediscover the principles for functioning in that truth!

According to Paul, every assembly is called to express the body of Christ locally by manifesting the character and power of Jesus. The functions of each assembly in achieving their purpose can only be accomplished through the gifts, ministries, and relational bonds established and empowered by the Spirit of God. Local oversight is the responsibility of a plural group of elders, who are Spirit-called men qualified foremost by godly character. Their purpose is to shepherd the assembly and equip each believer for his or her place of service in the body. At all times, the primary emphasis of the Church is the centrality of its Head, Jesus Christ.

The Glorious Church is a clear window of revelation into the mystery of Christ and His Church. The concepts and insights set forth will prove to be essential in preparing the 21st Century Church for the great end-time harvest, the spiritual warfare that is sure to arise, and the glorious return of the Lord Jesus.

Dale Rumble, Kingston, NY
Author of *The Diakonate* and
many other tremendous books

Foreword by Tony Tamel

One of the most profound proofs of God's existence is His Church. This community of citizens, called by and to Christ out of the world, has not only withstood the forces of Satan, it has also endured the handling of man. Although the Church has been influenced, manipulated, and exploited by unregenerated leaders throughout its history, she has remained God's only redemptive instrument on the face of the earth. The Almighty has kept His Church by His power for His purpose.

The Bible refers to this illustrious community of believers as the Bride and the Body of Christ. These names refer to her beauty and function, and nothing on the face of the earth compares to her. It is no wonder that God chose to inspire the writer of Ephesians to pen the word "glorious" in describing the Church. The strange irony is that the object of God's love and the means of accomplishing His will for all mankind is a mystery not only to the world, but also to the Church herself. While the world perceives her as being confused and ineffectual, she struggles with her own identity. She has failed to fully comprehend who she is, and why God has put her in the place of eminence. Once she finally grasps these mysteries, she will be prepared to utilize God's grace and power to fulfill her purpose.

In *The Glorious Church*, authors David Huston and Jim McKinley have done a superb job of describing God's purpose for the Church, as well as revealing her defining characteristics and how she is to operate in the world. To reveal these secrets withheld from the world, Huston and

McKinley use a contemporary interview with Paul, the apostle of Christ, to articulate answers concerning the Church. What better way to discover the truth about the Church than to inquire of the most prolific writer of the New Testament. Using this format, Paul elucidates his own letters to the churches of Asia, thus providing us with a clear and concise portrait of the Church.

The Glorious Church is certain to change the thinking of many about what God intends the Church to be and how she is to carry out her purpose. A clear understanding of these realities is what today's Church needs to be effectual in these last days. Get ready for a new Church paradigm.

Anthony Tamel, Oak Creek, WI
Pastor of a flourishing church
with over 100 home groups

I appreciate the chance to preview *The Glorious Church* dealing with church purpose and structure and presented as an interview with the apostle Paul. The writing itself represents a neat accomplishment that merits congratulations all its own.

Sidney Poe, Jackson, MS
College professor and
district Sunday school director

I just finished your booklet on *The Glorious Church*. It was well done and will certainly challenge many folks concerning the house God is building in our day.

Donald Rumble, Saugerties, NY
Local church elder and author of
Apostolic and Prophetic Foundations

I greatly enjoyed the substance of *The Glorious Church*. The format was fresh and almost entertaining, causing me to read it with a new interest and perspective. I would recommend it to anyone, young or old, new or mature Christian.

Owen Taylor, Annapolis, MD
Christian Freedom Foundation and
Apostolic Law Association

Greetings Fellow Believer,

The Bible tells us that when Jesus returns, He will present to Himself a "glorious church, not having spot or wrinkle or any such thing" (Ephesians 5:27). We believe that within the heart of every minister of the gospel is a deep longing to see the fullness of this glorious Church revealed in every local assembly.

The book you're holding was conceived out of an intense desire to gain a more perfect understanding of how God will bring forth this glorious Church. Our hope is that better understanding will unite with the desire to see His glory, bringing us closer to the fulfillment of God's eternal purpose.

In contemplating where to begin, we decided on the following scenario:

Imagine that God has personally invited you to obey His wonderful plan of salvation and you have responded with sincere and appreciative obedience. You don't know any other Christians, and you know nothing about any kind of church, church service, or church organization. Having provided you with a copy of His Word, God then asks you to describe His eternal purpose, the purpose of His Church, and how the localized expressions of His Church should be structured.

Before reading on, we ask you to stop to consider these significant questions. Suppose you knew nothing about church and knew no other Christians. All you had was the Bible and the Presence of God. If you are willing, take some time right now to ponder these questions:

1. **What is the eternal purpose of God?**
2. **What is the purpose of the Church?**
3. **How should a local assembly be structured to fulfill its purpose?**

We believe that you will gain more from this book if you first take time to grapple with these questions. If you would care to write out your responses, we are very interested in reading them. We recognize the limitations of our own understanding and plan to alter and refine this presentation as additional insight is provided on the three questions posed above. For this reason, we strongly encourage you to contact us with any comments, suggestions, and challenges you may have to any points we have made.

Your brothers in Jesus,
David Huston and Jim McKinley

A Look Back to the Future

Upon this rock I will build my church;
and the gates of hell shall not prevail against it.
Matthew 16:18, AV

What is the future of the Church and what will she look like? Can we know? Can we visualize her? Is it possible to describe the Church of the future? The answer is a resounding "yes!" And the reason we can say this is because the Bible describes the Church Jesus will present to Himself. It says He will come for a "glorious church, not having spot or wrinkle or any such thing, but that she should be holy and without blemish" (Ephesians 5:27). This is our future. It is divinely settled and unconditionally determined to come to pass.

But what does the Bible mean by the term "glorious Church?" How do we define it? How do we describe it? How do we really know if we are approaching it in our own experience within the body of Christ? We may convince ourselves that our local assembly is more glorious than the one in the town down the highway, but is this an accurate way of assessing our level of glory? Wouldn't it be more logical to evaluate a local assembly's glory by comparing it to the glorious Church of the New Testament.

As we read through the Epistles and the book of Acts, we see firsthand the church pattern established by Jesus. The Scriptures give us no basis for thinking that He ever intended His pattern to be altered or "improved upon" by those who came after the original apostles. The pattern Jesus established for His Church was to endure until the time of His coming.

During the past 1900 years, the original apostolic pattern has been distorted by the doctrinal, structural, and ministerial errors of a profusion of false teachers. Sadly, many sincere believers have uncritically accepted these errors resulting in a misshapen and often unproductive body. Even though much has been restored to date, it nevertheless remains impossible to accurately envision the glorious Church Jesus established by looking at the Church as it exists today. This means that we cannot know if we have a "glorious church" by comparing ourselves among ourselves. The only way to know, the only way to see the Church in its future state, is to look back to the original Church as described in the New Testament. The original is the pattern for the future.

Why is it important for us to accurately envision the glorious Church? The reason is simple: Jesus did not say that *we* would build His Church—He said that *He* would build it. The only Church that will prevail against the gates of hell (the grave) is the one He builds. Clearly we are His fellow-workers, but He is the Ultimate Builder. He owns the Church because He purchased it with His own blood. He designed it, He selects the materials for it, and He directs its construction. All attempts to build His Church without knowing how He envisions it are like building a house without looking at the blueprints. As the psalmist declared, "Unless the LORD builds the house, they labor in vain who build it" (Psalms 127:1). The time is too short for vain laboring. We must have accurate vision.

Paul wrote that each laborer will receive a reward from

Jesus according to how well their work in building the Church endures the testing of fire. If our work fails the test, we will suffer loss, though we can still be saved. But there's more to entering eternity than simply being saved. Let us reflect on how we can do the best work possible. As Paul admonished, we must "each one take heed how he builds" (1 Corinthians 3:10).

If we are to labor effectively with Jesus as He builds the "glorious church without spot or wrinkle," we must see the Church as He sees her. To do this, we must have accurate spiritual vision. But before we can accurately envision the Church, we must first be clear as to her purpose. The Greek word translated "purpose" in the New Testament literally means "something laid out in advance." Based on this definition, we will consider purpose to have the following meaning:

> *PURPOSE: The original intent of an object from its creation.*

What was God's original intent for the Church? By focusing on this question, by looking back in time to the origin of the Church, we can discover the answer to the question, *What is the future of the Church?* As we begin to more clearly envision the future "glorious Church," we will be better able to accurately evaluate the present state of glory in our local assemblies. Even more importantly, we will begin to see where God desires to take His Church in the days leading up to His great and glorious appearing.

What you are about to read is a contemporary interview with Paul, the bondservant and apostle of Jesus Christ. We acknowledge that we have taken a great liberty in presenting our ideas in this manner, running the risk that some may think us presumptuous, putting words in the mouth of the great apostle. We simply ask the reader to accept this interview format as no more than a useful literary device, enabling us to discuss or explain important biblical concepts in an interesting way. If you disagree with any of our points or believe we have put in Paul's mouth ideas he would never have uttered, we respect your views and ask you to bring these ideas to our attention.

A Contemporary Interview with Paul

Imagine that Paul, the bondservant and apostle of Jesus Christ, has stepped out of the first century and into the twenty-first. He now speaks to us as the consummate teacher, preacher, church planter, apostle, and man of God. He speaks to us out of His first century experiences and his twenty-first century observations. He takes us into the past that we might behold the future and shows us where we are going by showing us where we began. Paul, the visionary, is a man of both past and future glories. There is none more qualified to speak to us of the past, that we might comprehend and prepare for the future.

Purpose

Interviewer: You have described yourself as a "wise master builder" (1 Corinthians 3:10). Tell us how you came to understand the structure Jesus intends for His Church.

Paul: With God, *structure always follows purpose*. He never makes something and then asks, "What can this be used for?" He first determines what He wants to accomplish, then makes something that is perfectly suited for His specific purpose. When we think of purpose, we should think of God's plan for an object—His original intent when He made it.

Interviewer: Can you give us an example of this?

Paul: Yes. The creation is an excellent example of this principle. In the beginning, God formed the earth in a logical, systematic fashion. He began by establishing the foundations, and then, day by day, added its furnishings, accessories, and finally its inhabitants. Isaiah tells us that the Lord formed the earth *to be inhabited* (Isaiah 45:18). This informs us as to His purpose, at least His initial purpose, in putting this planet together. It was to serve as a habitation for man. Having established this as the purpose, the structure was consequently established. In other words, if His purpose had been to make a place solely for birds to inhabit, the structure would have been different. But since He was making a place for man, this purpose determined everything concerning the structure of its layout, its furnishings, and its accessories.

Interviewer: So you are saying that because God's purpose was to make a suitable place for man to dwell, He formed the earth as it presently is?

Paul: No. Not exactly. The way we see the earth now is not the way it was when God first formed it. Don't forget that there was a time when there was no sin in the world. After sin entered the world, God altered the structure of the earth to accommodate His purpose.

Interviewer: Please tell us more about God's purpose.

Paul: From the beginning, God's purpose has been to live within His creation in close fellowship with the creatures He made in His own image—in other words, with man. The garden of Eden was perfectly designed to accommodate this purpose: it was pure and sinless, and radiant with the glory of God. Here God and man lived together in perfect unity.

After man sinned, however, the structure of the earth changed. Since God no longer lived in unity with man, and since the earth was no longer a place of sinless purity, and since the glory of God no longer filled the earth, God set about restoring and perfecting His creation. This was His plan from the beginning, which is why Habakkuk the prophet declared, *For the earth will be filled with the knowledge of the glory of the LORD, as the waters cover the sea* (2:14). The state of man's present existence reflects God's purpose to bring all things into the fulfillment of their original intent. This is called perfection. Once the creation is finally brought into this glorious state, it will be forever protected from the destructive forces of sin.

Interviewer: You say that in its original condition, the creation was filled with the glory of God. Talk to us about the glory of God. What is it? How are we to understand it?

Paul: Throughout the Scriptures, the word "glory" is used to describe the invisible God making Himself visible or perceivable—and therefore knowable. Since God is not a deceiver, He only manifests Himself as He really is. This means that the glory of God is simply...God.

The concept of the glory of God is closely tied to the idea of the knowledge of God. While *glory* pertains to God making Himself known, *knowledge* pertains to His relationship with those who have come to know Him. To know God means to be in personal relationship with Him. According to the Scriptures, God has a plan to reveal Himself to everyone on earth and bring those who come to Him into personal relationship with Him. As this occurs, the earth will once again be filled with the knowledge of the glory of the Lord.

The Plan

Interviewer: How long has mankind been aware of God's plan to restore and perfect His creation?

Paul: This is impossible to know exactly. We do know that at the time of Israel's deliverance from Egypt, God talked to Moses about His plan. According to the Scriptures, when the people rebelled against God in the wilderness, He decided to destroy them and start over with the descendants of Moses. After Moses pleaded with God to spare the people, the Lord relented and allowed them to continue on their way to the Promised Land. He then declared His purpose to Moses, saying, *"Truly, as I live, all the earth shall be filled with the glory of the LORD"* (Numbers 14:21).

Interviewer: God has been dealing with mankind for nearly 6000 years now and the earth is not yet filled with His glory. Why hasn't He accomplished His goal?

Paul: Stated simply, mankind in general has not cooperated. The important thing we must always remember is that ultimately nothing will prevent God from accomplishing His purpose; however, since the day Adam and Eve disobeyed God in the garden, the rebellion of man has stood as an impediment to the full and perfect radiance of His glory. Knowing in advance that man would sin, God took this factor into consideration when He devised His plan, making provision for dealing with this impediment justly and completely. Here we observe the mighty power of the glory of God. It is His glory that eradicates sin. God has never desired to do away with man, only the sin of man. It is only man's defiance of the will of God that, from our perspective, impedes the fulfillment of His purpose.

Interviewer: What do you mean when you say His glory eradicates sin?

Paul: Just as light eradicates darkness, so God's glory eradicates sin.

Interviewer: Please explain how God brings His glory into this sin-stained creation.

Paul: Let me confine my explanation to the New Testament context. The Scriptures tell us that in the process of time, God announced the forthcoming arrival of His glory by the voice of one crying in the wilderness: *"Prepare the way of the LORD"* (Isaiah 40:3). This of course was John the Baptist, who proclaimed, *"The glory of the LORD shall be revealed, and all flesh shall see it together"* (Isaiah 40:5; Luke 3:4-6).

The revelation of the glory of the Lord to all flesh was accomplished by the coming of Jesus the Messiah. As my fellow apostle John declared, *And the Word became flesh and dwelt among us, and we beheld His glory...full of grace and truth* (John 1:14). This event is what I was referring to when I wrote, *God was manifested in the flesh* (1 Timothy 3:16).

Interviewer: Please tell us more about this *Word* that became flesh?

Paul: The *Word* that became flesh is the same *Word* that was *in the beginning.* It is the same *Word* that *was with God* and *was God* (John 1:1). The Greek word John uses here is *logos,* which can be defined as "a logical expression of ideas; a plan." In other words, what the Lord wants us to know is that from the very beginning He has had a plan. The plan was "with" Him, that is, it was in His heart. And even more remarkably, the plan "was" Him, because the plan was that He would be glorified in His creation.

Interviewer: So you are saying that God's plan, which He had from the beginning, became flesh; and that is who Jesus the Messiah is. And you are also saying that this incarnate plan is the glory of God.

Paul: Exactly! When the preordained time arrived, the plan was put into action: the plan became flesh, walked the earth, taught the truth, healed the sick, and ultimately bore the sins of the world on the cross of Calvary. This is why those who saw Jesus could say, "And we beheld His glory." And since "glory" is the invisible God making Himself visible to His creation, we can say that God was manifested, or made visible, in the flesh.

And this manifested God eradicated the sin and rebellion of man as an impediment to the fulfillment of His plan. This is why Jesus said on the night of His arrest, *"I have glorified You on the earth. I have finished the work which You have given Me to do"* (John 17:4). The Messiah considered His primary work to be that of glorifying the invisible God on the earth. And it was through this work that sin was destroyed, for John writes, *For this purpose the Son of God was manifested, that He might destroy the works of the devil* (1 John 3:8).

God's Pattern

Interviewer: Why do you think God chose the Incarnation as the New Testament form for His glory?

Paul: It is important to understand that God is separate and distinct from His physical creation. In the present age, He has determined that He will make Himself known by means of an earthly physical structure. This way, He can make Himself known while simultaneously keeping Himself hidden.

Interviewer: Explain what you mean when you say He

can make Himself known while simultaneously keeping Himself hidden?

Paul: Whenever God inhabits an earthly structure, some will see the God who is in the structure while others will see only the structure. For example, Thomas looked at Jesus and said, "My Lord and my God," while Pilate looked at the very same person and said, "Behold the man" (John 20:28; 19:5). One saw God, the other saw only the earthly structure —the man. This is how God can be present with everyone yet known only to those who have a heart to see Him.

Interviewer: This is interesting. Can you give us another example of God's earthly structure?

Paul: In the Old Testament period, God's earthly structure was first called the tabernacle and later the temple. When He gave instructions to the builders of these structures, He made it clear they were to build *according to the pattern which you were shown* (Exodus 26:30). The Hebrew word for "pattern" refers to an official decree, in this case a decree issued by God Himself. The builders had no voice or vote in the design of the structure. The purpose of God determined and defined the design.

Interviewer: So the structure was determined by the purpose God intended for it and therefore had to be built according to the pattern God showed them.

Paul: Yes, that is correct. Now let me bring this idea into the New Testament. Isaiah wrote, *For the earth shall be full of the knowledge of the LORD as the waters cover the sea. And in that day there shall be a Root of Jesse, who* *shall stand as a banner to the people; for the Gentiles shall seek Him, and His resting place shall be glorious* (Isaiah 11:9-10). This *Root of Jesse* who shall stand as a banner is Jesus the Messiah. The Hebrew word translated "banner" comes from a word that means "to gleam from afar; to be conspicuous as a signal." The Scriptures often depict the glory of God as being like a bright light, bathing the earth with its brilliance.

The *glorious resting place* of Jesus is the earthly structure, built and prepared by Him in partnership with us, His fellow workmen, to serve as the dwelling place of God on the earth. David described this structure when he wrote, *For the LORD has chosen Zion; He has desired it for His dwelling place: "This is My resting place forever; here I will dwell, for I have desired it"* (Psalms 132:13-14). In its initial fulfillment, this passage refers to Mt. Zion, the site of Solomon's temple during the Old Testament period. Mt. Zion is also a title for the Church, for we have come to *Mount Zion and to the city of the living God, the heavenly Jerusalem...to the general assembly and church* (Hebrews 12:22-23).

Interviewer: So you're saying that the Church is the structure God inhabits today?

Paul: Yes. The Church has always been the heart and soul of God's plan. From the beginning God has desired a glorious Church, a living temple in which He can dwell and through which He can shine forth in glory. This temple is being constructed of men and woman, purified from sin by the blood of Jesus Christ, and built together according to God's pattern into a holy habitation of God. It is manifested in the earth as localized assemblies which are established and periodically strengthened by various trans-local ministries.

God's Eternal Purpose

Interviewer: Based on everything you have told us thus far, how would you describe the ultimate, eternal purpose of God?

Paul: God's eternal purpose is: *To purify His creation and bring it into perfect unity, that the earth would be eternally filled with His glory.*

Interviewer: What are the key elements of this purpose?

Paul: The key elements of God's purpose are **PURITY, UNITY,** and **GLORY.** Purity refers to being in a sinless, undefiled condition, which is the condition God is always in. Unity refers to the personal relationships which bind men together with one another and with God. Glory refers to God making Himself known in His creation.

Interviewer: Can you refer us to some passages of Scripture that speak specifically about these elements? Perhaps some of your own writings?

Paul: Yes. The first three chapters of my letter to the Ephesians constitute an essay on the eternal purpose of God. Let me walk you through several key portions. In the first chapter I write: *Just as He chose us in Him before the foundation of the world...* (Ephesians 1:4a). Here I introduce the idea of purpose, God's original intent for the Church. He established His purpose before He began to create.

That we should be holy and without blame before Him in love... (1:4b). Here I introduce the idea of purity, which is a vital component of our relationship with God. For us to relate to a pure God, we must be pure as well. Of course, our purity is not a product of our compliance with law, but a product of His cleansing us from sin. I do not mean by this that human purity is only a theological condition with no practical reality. Quite the contrary. Even though our purity comes through the cleansing of Messiah's blood, we must actively purify ourselves by *obeying the truth* (1 Peter 1:22).

I then write, *Having predestined us to adoption as sons by Jesus Christ to Himself, according to the good pleasure of His will...* (1:5). God determined in advance that He would adopt us into personal relationship with Himself through the Messiah. This is not something He does because He is obligated to; He does it because it is His good pleasure to do so. It is His purpose.

And He does all this for us *to the praise of the glory of His grace, by which He has made us accepted in the Beloved...* (1:5). We are made acceptable to God in the Messiah by God's grace, His kindness, not because of our own good conduct. We enter into relationship with Him, not because we are good, but because He is good. For this we ought to praise the glory of His grace, thereby making Him known not just as God, but as the God who is good.

Interviewer: Can you help us to envision the fulfillment of God's purpose?

Paul: Yes. John provided us with a marvelous portrait of the ultimate fulfillment of God's purpose when he wrote, *Then one of the seven angels...came to me and talked with me, saying, "Come, I will show you the bride, the Lamb's wife"* (Revelation 21:9). John described the Church as the Lamb's wife. This denotes both purity and unity, for the bride of Messiah will certainly be chaste and without blemish; moreover, she will be united with Him in an unending intimate relationship. He then described her as *having the glory of God* (21:11). In other words, she will know God as He really is.

In the first chapter of my letter to the Ephesians, I write, *Having made known to us the mystery of His will, according to His good pleasure which He purposed in Himself, that in the dispensation of the fullness of the times He might gather together in one all things in Christ, both which are in heaven and which are on earth; in Him* (1:9-10). Here is God's purpose clearly summarized as a gathering together of all things in Christ.

Interviewer: When God's purpose is fulfilled, will disunity be a thing of the past?

Paul: That is correct. A recent English translation called *The New International Version* translates this passage this way: *And he made known to us the mystery of his will...to bring all things in heaven and on earth together under one head, even Christ.* Another translation, *The New English Bible* says it even more powerfully: *He has made known to us His hidden purpose...namely, that the universe, all in* *heaven and on earth, might be brought into a unity in Christ.* Satan is the author of corruption and division. God's purpose is to destroy the works of the devil and restore His creation to purity and unity, that His glory would fill the earth.

I then wrote, *In Him also we have obtained an inheritance, being predestined according to the purpose of Him who works all things according to the counsel of His will, that we who first trusted in Christ should be to the praise of His glory* (Ephesians 1:11-12). Those of us who have trusted in Messiah, that is, who have entered into relationship with Him, have been predestined according to His purpose to be to the praise of His glory, for we shall *shine forth as the sun, like the brightness of the firmament* (Matthew 13:43; Daniel 12:3). This will happen when Jesus comes to be *glorified in His saints and to be admired among all those who believe* (2 Thessalonians 1:10).

God's Purpose and the Gospel

Interviewer: You have said that God's purpose is to live in eternal union with those He brings to Himself, that is, His Church, but that the Church is also the means through which the glory of God fills the earth. Is the Church the object of God's purpose or the means through which He accomplishes His purpose?

Paul: The Church is both. She is the object of God's purpose, because His desire is to live in eternal union with His Church. But she is also the means by which He is bringing this purpose to pass. And this is where the gospel comes in.

Interviewer: Please explain what you mean about the gospel.

Paul: God is fulfilling His purpose by first reconciling man to Himself through the gospel, and then, living in intimate relationship with those He has reconciled. The very nature of this relationship—man living in union with God—transforms man into the glorious image of Messiah, which allows God's glory to shine.

I expressed these ideas in my second letter to the Corinthians when I wrote to them saying, *Lest the light of the gospel of the glory of Christ, who is the image of God, should shine on them. For we do not preach ourselves, but Christ Jesus the Lord, and ourselves your bondservants for Jesus' sake. For it is the God who commanded light to shine out of darkness, who has shone in our hearts to give the light of the knowledge of the glory of God in the face of Jesus Christ* (4:4-6).

Habakkuk stated unequivocally that the knowledge of God's glory would *fill the earth.* But how will this happen? The answer is through the preaching of the gospel of the glory of Christ. When asked when the end of this age would come, the Lord Himself said, *"And this gospel of the kingdom will be preached in all the world as a witness to all the nations, and then the end will come"* (Matthew 24:14). The Church must be about the work of preaching the gospel right up to the time of His coming. Why? This is how God is fulfilling His purpose to **PURIFY His creation and bring it into perfect UNITY,**

that the earth would be eternally filled with His
GLORY.

Interviewer: Are you saying that the preaching of the
gospel by God's people is the shining forth of the light of
the knowledge of the glory of God?

Paul: Yes, exactly. But let me take you back to my letter to
the Ephesians. In the third chapter I wrote, *To the intent
that now the manifold wisdom of God might be made known
by the church*—this is God making Himself known through
the Church as we are transformed into His image and as
we preach the glorious gospel. In this case He is being
revealed to *the principalities and powers in the heavenly
places*—these are the spiritual forces that foment sin and
undermine the unity of the body of Christ. All this is done
*according to the eternal purpose which He accomplished in
Christ Jesus our Lord* (3:10-11).

God accomplished His purpose in the Messiah through
His death, burial, and resurrection. But it remains for the
Church to manifest the fulfillment of this purpose.

Interviewer: Do I hear you saying that Jesus has made
provision for everything the Church needs to accomplish
her purpose, but that it's now up to the Church to finish
the work He has brought her forth to do?

Paul: That is correct. Although let me quickly add that it is
not His intention that we build apart from His direction
as the Head of the body. He is with us. He is connected
to us. We are *bone of His bone and flesh of His flesh*. He is
our power, our wisdom, our enablement. Without Him
we can do nothing, but with Him all things are possible.

Understanding this should not diminish our desire to work, it should enhance it. We should be inspired to work all the more because we know He is leading us toward His purpose.

Interviewer: Just so we are all clear on God's eternal purpose, could you summarize it once again, perhaps in a little more detail?

Paul: God's eternal purpose is:

> *To establish a dwelling place out of reconciled and purified men and women who are united with one another and with God by spiritual relationships. It will be among these people that God will enjoy eternal fellowship with mankind and will show forth the fulness of His glory throughout His creation.*

I closed the third chapter of my letter to the Ephesians with these words: *To Him be glory in the church by Christ Jesus to all generations, forever and ever. Amen* (Ephesians 3:21). It is vital for us to see that the purpose of God is that His glory would fill the earth. The exclusive structure through which His glory will shine is the Church— Jesus being the Head and each of us members individually.

The Purpose of the Church

Interviewer: We began this interview by talking about the structure of the Church. This led directly into a discussion of God's plan to reveal Himself and His eternal purpose. The following question seems in order at this point in our discussion: What is the purpose of the Church, this corporate body of true believers?

Paul: God does not operate primarily for our sake; He operates for His own sake. Therefore, we cannot know the purpose of the Church apart from knowing the eternal purpose of God. The purpose of the Church is always subject to the purpose of God.

Based on what we know to be the purpose of God, we can describe the purpose of the Church as follows: *To live in intimate relationship with God, providing Him a purified body through which His glory can shine throughout the earth.* In the end, our purpose is to glorify God.

Interviewer: What can you point to in the Scriptures to show us this purpose?

Paul: I can point to Jesus. He is the pattern for the Church. By living out His life on earth, He exemplified as one individual how we, as His corporate body, are to live and order our priorities. One thing that becomes obvious upon reading through the Gospels is that Jesus lived for a higher purpose than other men. While most men live for their own glory, Jesus lived for the glory of God. As I said earlier, He considered His work to be that of glorifying God.

Interviewer: How did Jesus accomplish this purpose?

Paul: By living in union with the Father, by faithful prayer, by purity of life, and by proclamation of the truth. He did all of this in an overarching spirit of sacrifice, a spirit that culminated in His humiliating death on the cross. In fact, on the eve of His death, Jesus prayed, *"Sanctify them by Your truth*—He prayed for our purity—*and the glory which You gave Me I have given them...that they may be made perfect in one*—He prayed for our unity—*and that the world may know that You have sent Me"*—He prayed that the glory of God would fill the earth (John 17:17, 21, 22).

After finishing this prayer, Jesus *loved the church and gave Himself for her* on the cross, *that He might sanctify and cleanse her with the washing of water by the word*—this was our purifying—*that He might present her to Himself* —our unifying—*a glorious church*—our glorifying (Ephesians 5:25-27). Purifying, unifying, and glorifying—that is what the Lord's purpose, and therefore the Church's purpose, is all about.

The Headship of Jesus

Interviewer: What must be in place for the Church to accomplish her purpose? I mean, are there any absolutes, any non-negotiables?

Paul: The answer to your question is an unequivocal YES! For the Church to accomplish her purpose, *Jesus Christ must be the functioning Head of the Church.*

Interviewer: Would you explain what you mean by "functioning Head?"

Paul: I mean we must be very careful not to give lip service to the idea of Jesus being Head of the Church. The Headship of Jesus is not intended to be some high-sounding theological concept; He intends it to be a living reality in the Church. This is why I don't stop at saying Jesus must *be* the Head of the Church. He *is* the Head by God's appointment. But for the Church to fulfill her purpose, Jesus must actually function as the Head.

Interviewer: So you're saying that even though Jesus has been *appointed* by God as Head of the Church, the Church may not in actuality be *functioning* under His Headship?

Paul: Precisely. As you know, there are many believers who mistakenly assume that confessing Jesus as Lord is the same as allowing Him to function as the Lord of their lives. Let me make this clear: Jesus Christ is, and always has been, the King of kings and the Lord of lords. His Lordship is unconditional. Regardless of whether a person acknowledges His Lordship and chooses to be in relationship with Him or not, He is still that person's Lord. But for Jesus to actually function as Lord, believers must freely submit to Him. Jesus Himself has warned that confession of His Lordship without submission is inadequate, saying, *"Why do you call Me 'Lord, Lord,' and do not do the things which I say?"* (Luke 6:46).

Interviewer: You seem to be making a distinction between the Lordship of Jesus and the Headship of Jesus. Is this right?

Paul: Yes. There is a fundamental difference between Lordship and Headship. The Lordship of Jesus Christ applies to the entire creation; He is Lord of all. His

Headship, however, applies only to the Church, for God *gave Him to be **head** over all things **to the church**, which is His body, the fullness of Him who fills all in all* (Ephesians 1:22-23). Lordship points to the submission and obedience of the individual believer. He rules us as Lord individually. Headship refers to the corporate relationship with Jesus. As the Head, he provides for and directs the body of believers. In local assemblies, the ascension-gift ministries (of Ephesians 4:11) are an interface between the Head and the body.

The significance of Jesus being the Head is that all life, all anointing, all ministry, all direction begin in Him and flow out to the appropriate members in the Church. An organism can have only one head, and these life functions of the head cannot be delegated to others, although in the plan of God, the oversight and equipping functions flow out from the Head through the ascension-gift ministries.

Headship also pertains to origins and authority. For example, the head of a river is the place where the river originates. Also, as the head of his household, a man exercises certain authority over his wife and children for their good and for their protection. These concepts were established in the very beginning. For example, just as Eve was brought forth from the side of Adam, the Church has been brought forth from Jesus Christ. He is the originator of the Church, and therefore her Head. And just as God specifically told Eve that her husband would rule over her, Paul tells us that the Church is to be subject to Jesus as her Head.

There can be no functional Headship over the body if there is no functional Lordship over the individual members. The Originator has full authority over what He has brought forth, for He nourishes and cherishes what He has brought forth.

Interviewer: What happens when a believer does not allow Jesus to function as the Lord of his life?

Paul: The Lordship of Jesus is directly related to His role as Savior. If He is to function as our Savior, He must also be allowed to function as our Lord. Jesus said, *"Not everyone who says to Me, 'Lord, Lord,' shall enter the kingdom of heaven, but he who does the will of My Father in heaven"* (Matthew 7:21). If we won't make His will for us the highest priority in our lives, we have no hope of living with Him for eternity. Submitting to His Lordship keeps us from going our own way and being lost. Any diminishing of Jesus' Lordship in a believer's life automatically results in diminished Headship in His body. How can the body accurately represent the thoughts and desires of the Head if the individual members are not yielded to Him? And the fact is, people are no more yielded to their spiritual leaders than they are to Jesus, the Head. When God's people are out of submission, Headship is misrepresented.

Interviewer: But doesn't Jesus need His body to accomplish His purpose?

Paul: Yes—which is why we must understand that when members are in effect usurping the authority of Jesus over His body, the body cannot fulfill His purpose in the earth. No Lordship, no Headship. No Headship, no purpose. When the members are not yielded to Jesus as the Head of the body, the Church loses its purpose for existing and becomes a directionless body, detached from the only source of power that can provide it with growth and glory.

The Headship of Christ should be seen as an *interdependent relationship* based on the authority of Jesus and the submission of the Church to His authority. Just as our human body must be attached to our head and is dependent upon it for life and direction, so must the Church remain attached to Jesus at all times. Conversely, if a head has no functioning body, it is unable to accomplish its purpose. Jesus is dependent on the Church to fulfill His purpose. But the Church is dependent on Jesus for its very life.

As the Head exercises authority and the body submits to that authority, the body of Christ functions as a living and glorious Church. Just as a human body is the means by which its head gives active expression to its thoughts and intents, so the Church is the means by which Jesus expresses Himself on the earth. And just as a human body enables its head to go wherever it wants to, so the Church enables Jesus to go where He wants to go. We are His feet and legs.

Interviewer: As a practical matter, what must the Church do to express the living Headship of Jesus?

Paul: For the Church to function freely as the living body of Jesus, each individual member must be yielded to Him as Lord. In other words, each member must be willing to do whatever Jesus asks of him. When the Lordship of Jesus is rejected, the members of the Church are governed by rules, traditions, and human control. Under this system, functional Headship is either greatly diminished or absent all together. Any human control and any rule or tradition that contradicts biblical principles prevents the body from operating freely under the direction of its Head. When the body is disconnected from the Head, it is forced to attempt to build itself up using humanly contrived programs. But the ministry of a local assembly should not be defined by programs; it should be defined by God's purpose and principles.

I'm not saying this is an all or nothing situation—total Headship versus no Headship. The degree of Headship being expressed in any local assembly will be determined by the degree the individual members are yielded to Jesus as Lord. The more who yield and the more yielded they are, the more the body will function under Jesus as the Head.

In most cases, rules and programs actually hinder the functioning of Jesus' Headship because they don't depend on submission to Him as Lord. They only require compliance with the rules or participation in the program. Moreover, rules and programs can actually inhibit growth, though they may appear to be producing growth in the short-term. But the biblical reality is, where there is no submission there is no relationship, and where there is no relationship, genuine growth is impossible. The growth of the body is the fruit of personal relationship.

Interviewer: Is there anything else the Church must do to have functional Headship?

Paul: Yes. A critical factor in establishing the functional Headship of Jesus in a local assembly is correct leadership structure. Even if everyone is yielded to Jesus as Lord, if a local assembly does not recognize all gifts and ministries of the Holy Spirit or fails to structure its governing ministry along biblical principles, the functional Headship of Jesus is either diminished or eliminated.

The oversight and equipping ministries operating in a local church are the earthly representations of the Head's oversight and equipping ministries to the Church. These ministries must operate in a spirit of serving and must be accepted, respected, and followed by the members of the local body. A cooperative attitude in both directions is vital.

Interviewer: So then, as members of the body of Christ, each one of us must accept our responsibility to keep ourselves connected and yielded to the Head in an intimate, personal relationship. And we do this by yielding to Jesus as our Lord and by cooperating with the spiritually-gifted and appointed leaders of our local assemblies. What is the result when Jesus is functioning as Head?

Paul: The result is growth! There are three principles pertaining to Headship that must be in place if a local assembly is to grow. I taught these principles to the church in Colossae when I wrote about *holding fast to the Head, from whom all the body, nourished and knit together by joints and ligaments, grows with the increase that is from God* (Colossians 2:19).

Interviewer: Explain what you mean by "holding fast to the Head"?

Paul: The literal meaning of "holding fast" is *to seize or to* *lay hold of.* I can't emphasize enough the importance of every member of the Church accepting their responsibility to do this. When even one member turns loose of Jesus, His functional Headship is diminished, if only slightly. He is the Head, but due to the diminished or broken connection with part His of body, He is less able to function as the Head. When this occurs, the body becomes either spastic (operating independent of the Head) or paralyzed (not operating at all). In either case, the body is not adequately hearing and doing what its Head is saying.

Interviewer: You said that it is from the Head that the body is *nourished and knit together.* What do you mean by this?

Paul: We are spiritually nourished by the Word of God. This is our bread, our meat. I refer here to the living Word, not the dead letter. We are knit together by the love of God, which is shed abroad in our hearts by the Holy Spirit. We are knit together as one body by the one Spirit that dwells within us. Both the Spirit and the living Word flow out of Jesus into His body.

When the body becomes disconnected from its Head, standards of conduct and clever programs are commonly substituted for the Headship of Jesus. This is man's attempt to produce glory and growth in a local assembly. But this is not God's way. For a season these standards and programs may appear to produce the right results. People may seem to be purified and the assembly may appear to be growing. But Jesus stated clearly that *without Him we can do nothing* (John 15:5). Just as a branch must be connected to the tree to produce fruit, so must we hold fast to the Head, being nourished with His

Word and knit together by His Spirit. Jesus is the builder of the Church. And He wants His house built according to His specifications because He's going to live in it for eternity!

Interviewer: What then are some practical ways to stay connected to Jesus as the Head of the Church?

Paul: When I wrote to the Colossians, I explained to them in detail what I had first given them in principle. I told them to *continue earnestly in prayer, being vigilant in it with thanksgiving...* (Colossians 4:2). This is the practical application of holding fast to the Head. I also told them, *Let the word of Christ dwell in you richly...* (Colossians 3:16). This is the practical application of being nourished with the Word.

I then exhorted them to *put on tender mercies, kindness, humility, meekness, longsuffering; bearing with one another, and forgiving one another, if anyone has a complaint against another; even as Christ forgave you, so you also must do. But above all these things put on love, which is the bond of perfection* (Colossians 3:12-14). The Spirit of God has no power to unite the body unless the members yield themselves to the outward expressions of the Spirit. What I have described here are the outward expressions of the Spirit in the relationships between God's people. This is what knits or binds the body together.

Interviewer: I notice that each of these principles pertains to what *we* must do, not what we should look to Jesus to do.

Paul: You are not only correct, but you have succinctly stated the key point. We must pray—no one can do that for us. We must learn the Word—no one can do that for us. And we must love our brothers and sisters with Christlike love. Each of these practices are our personal responsibilities as members of the Lord's body. No one can do them for us—we must do them for ourselves. As the members of a local body begin to put these principles into practice, Jesus will begin to function as the Head of the Church and the Church will be able to fulfill its purpose in the earth.

These principles were established in the beginning as the core practices of the original Church. As soon as the baptisms of Pentecost were completed, the Church *continued steadfastly in the apostles' doctrine* [this is the nourishment of the Word] *and fellowship, in the breaking of bread* [this describes the body being knit together], *and in prayers* [prayer is the primary means by which we hold fast to the Head]. And what did Jesus as the Head do in response? *The Lord added to the church daily those who were being saved* (Acts 2:42, 47). Just as He promised, God gave the increase!

The Priority of Prayer

Interviewer: If you had to boil all this down to one word, what would that word be?

Paul: Without question, that word is *PRAYER!*

Interviewer: So prayer is the number one priority in a Christian's life?

Paul: Yes. Prayer must be the highest priority for every believer. It is the *one needful thing* Jesus spoke of in Luke 10:42. In Luke 18 He taught that *men ought always to pray and not lose heart.* In my letter to the church in Thessalonica, I admonished the saints to *pray without ceasing* (1 Thessalonians 5:17). Prayer is not just vital, it is irreplaceable. A church that doesn't pray is like an electrical appliance that has not been plugged into the power source. The appliance may be perfectly constructed, but if it isn't plugged in, it can't fulfill its purpose. The same is true for the Church.

Interviewer: If prayer is so essential, why is it so lacking?

Paul: Prayer is lacking for two primary reasons: First, many believers don't understand why they should pray. They think of it as little more than a way of getting things from God. Second, many have never been taught how to pray effectively; therefore, they fail to pray consistently. Without prayer there can be no genuine relationship with Jesus. Man connects with God through prayer. Jesus imparts His thoughts and directives to His people through prayer. Jesus empowers His people to do His will through prayer. Prayer is our connection with Jesus, the Lord of our lives and the Head of His Church.

Prayer is the primary means for establishing and preserving the Headship of Jesus Christ in the Church. If a believer doesn't pray, he is, in effect, displacing Jesus as the Lord of his life and preventing Him from functioning as the Head of one member of His body.

Interviewer: This sounds serious! How can believers be encouraged to pray more consistently and effectively?

Paul: Two things need to happen. First, believers need to recognize more acutely their utter dependence on Jesus. The Lord told His disciples this very plainly just before His crucifixion when He said, *"I am the vine, you are the branches. He who abides in Me, and I in him, bears much fruit; for without Me you can do nothing."* (John 15:5). Did you hear that word? He said, *nothing.* Just as a branch must be attached to the vine, if we are to bear fruit, we must be attached to Jesus.

I told the Corinthians the same thing in my second letter when I said, *Not that we are sufficient of ourselves to think of anything as being from ourselves, but our sufficiency is from God.* (2 Corinthians 3:5). Apart from Jesus Christ, we can accomplish nothing of eternal value—we just don't have the wherewithal. Our sufficiency is entirely and exclusively from Him. When we cease to pray and start depending solely on our own ingenuity, our own strengths, our own will power, we cut off the voice of the only One who is able to accomplish His purpose in the earth. We cannot accomplish it on our own; we can only accomplish it by working *with* Him.

Interviewer: You are certainly zealous about prayer.

Paul: When it comes to believers dethroning Jesus as the Lord of their lives, I'll become even more zealous than this. Failing to pray opens the door to sin. For the Church to be pure, knit together in love, and full of the glory of God, she must be a praying Church.

Interviewer: Which fulfills the three key elements of God's purpose, right?

Paul: Precisely.

Interviewer: What is the second thing that needs to happen for believers to start praying more effectively?

Paul: They must understand that prayer is not a religious ritual. The formalities of prayer—flowery language, volume, body position, location, duration—these things are not what make prayer effective. None of these are related to the true purpose of prayer. It is the attitude of the one doing the praying that makes prayer effective. As James said, *The effective, fervent prayer of a righteous man avails much* (James 5:16). He didn't say a thing about formalities, volume, or wordiness.

Jesus crystallized this truth when He said, *God is Spirit, and those who worship Him must worship in spirit and truth* (John 4:24). Worship, spirit, truth—these words indicate the heart attitude of prayer, not the superfluous technicalities of prayer.

Interviewer: This saying of Jesus is often quoted but seemingly misunderstood. Before we leave this point, would you delve a little deeper into what Jesus means when He speaks about worshiping in spirit and in truth?

Paul: This passage is replete with great spiritual truths. In the Greek language the word translated "worship" (*proskuneo*, #4352) literally means to kiss, like the way a dog licks his master's hand. It can also mean to fawn or crouch, or to prostrate oneself in homage, either literally or figuratively. It is often used in connection with reverence and adoration, especially for God.

By using this word, Jesus was making the point that believers must be exceedingly and severely humble before God. Humility is the only proper attitude for prayer. To pray *in spirit* means that our prayer must come, not just from our lips, but also from our heart. There is nothing ceremonial or ritualistic about genuine prayer. It is far more than just reading or reciting prayers; it is communicating with God directly from the heart. As David wrote in the Psalms, *Blessed are those who keep His testimonies, who seek Him with the whole heart!* (Psalms 119:2).

To pray *in truth* means to recognize God in truth, that is, as He really is. This means understanding what the Bible says about God and worshiping Him according to the Scriptures, not according to our own ideas. David poetically captured this truth when He wrote, *The LORD is near to all who call upon Him, to all who call upon Him in truth* (Psalms 145:18).

Interviewer: So when a believer prays, he must have a humble attitude before the Lord, seek Him from his heart, and worship Him according to doctrinal truth.

Paul: No. There is more to "praying in truth" than simply understanding the doctrine of God. Praying in truth also means coming to God with an honest heart, not trying to hide any part of us, but exposing ourselves to God as we really are. David captured this powerful truth when he wrote, *LORD, who may abide in Your tabernacle? Who may dwell in Your holy hill? He who...speaks the truth in* *his heart* (Psalms 15:1-2). He also wrote, *Behold, You desire truth in the inward parts. Create in me a clean heart, O God.* (Psalms 51:6,10). If we are not completely honest with God, if we try to hide any corruption in our hearts, no matter how seemingly insignificant, we risk being cut off from the presence of God.

Interviewer: Complete honesty is a tall order, Paul.

Paul: Yes. Many people have a terrible struggle revealing the corruption of their hearts to the perfect and righteous God. But whenever we deny the truth about ourselves, we are also denying the truth about God. We are denying His mercy. We are saying we don't believe He can be trusted with the truth. Oh, let us see that His mercy is the only hope we have.

God is always honest about Himself with us, and He wants us to be honest about ourselves with Him. This is because He desires a real and open *relationship*. If you think about it, honesty is the most important ingredient in any close, personal relationship. It clears the way for genuine communication.

Truth is the vital ingredient in building strong bonds of trust between believers and God. Our willingness to confront the corruption within our hearts and present it to a just God brings reality to our relationship with Him. Through truth, we can know Him and He can know us.

Interviewer: Paul, is there ever a time when God does not hear our prayers?

Paul: Yes. The Scriptures are very clear about this. Man's relationship with God is based upon each party's position: Jesus is God, superior to us in every way, and we are man, entirely dependent upon Him for everything. He acknowledges us for who we are, and we must acknowledge Him for who He is. We acknowledge His Headship by hearing and obeying His voice. When we refuse, our prayers fall on deaf ears, so to speak.

Solomon confirms this when he writes that anyone who *turns away his ear from hearing the law, even his prayer is an abomination* (Proverbs 28:9). And David warned, *If I regard iniquity in my heart, the Lord will not hear* (Psalms 66:18). If we refuse to hear the Word of God and obey it, we lose our audience with the King. But when we keep our ears open to His voice, God's ears stay open to our voice.

Interviewer: This seems to circle back to what you said earlier about a person's attitude toward prayer.

Paul: Yes. We must be teachable, submissive, and above all, completely honest. Then God will hear our prayers. As John wrote, *Beloved, if our heart does not condemn us, we have confidence toward God. And whatever we ask we receive from Him, because we keep His commandments and do those things that are pleasing in His sight* (1 John 3:21-22). And David summed it up nicely when he wrote, *Teach me Your way, O LORD; I will walk in Your truth; unite my heart to fear Your name. I will praise You, O Lord my God, with all my heart, and I will glorify Your name forevermore* (Psalms 86:11-12). It's obvious, is it not, why David is remembered as the man after God's own heart.

Fulfilling God's Purpose

Interviewer: Paul, you have given us some very practical insights for the individual believer, but what about the local expression of the body of Christ? How does the *spirit and truth* principle apply to the purpose of a local assembly?

Paul: The Bible tells us that God's glory is *full of grace and truth* (John 1:14). It also tells us, as we were just discussing, that God is to be worshiped in *spirit and truth* (John 4:24). Truth is concrete and definitive. It refers to the form or structure of a thing. Grace and spirit, however, refer to the way a thing is used. For example, the same knife that can be used to graciously slice a piece of meat can also be used to viciously stab an innocent man. The truth, or structure, of the knife remains the same, but the spirit in which the knife is used changes from good to evil.

Interviewer: That illustration makes the difference between grace and truth very clear. Can we say that truth is the "what" and spirit is the "how?" How does this grace and truth concept apply to a local assembly?

Paul: Let me begin by saying that God has chosen the Church, as manifested in local expressions of His body, as the instrument through which His glory shines. The local assembly is responsible, therefore, for upholding the truth of God, or more precisely, the structure God intended for His body, and for ministering graciously in the spirit of Christ. We must glorify God the way He desires to be glorified. He does not present us with a series of options. God has established the way. He is the owner of the Church.

Interviewer: How can a local assembly achieve this balance between truth and spirit?

Paul: The only way any local assembly can achieve this balance is by fully committing to the purpose of God—so much so that when it realizes it is engaged in any activity that does not further the purpose of God, it stops it immediately. God is never pleased when what He created for a specific purpose is used for another purpose. Local assemblies must be committed to both fulfilling the purpose of God *and* fulfilling it in the way God intended it to be fulfilled. This commitment requires a willingness to make any necessary changes, regardless of how much those changes may cut against the grain of the status quo.

Interviewer: It seems to me, Paul, that this will require great courage.

Paul: I suppose it will. But we need to remember who it is we serve. *Or do I seek to please men? For if I still pleased men, I would not be a bondservant of Christ* (Galatians 1:10).

Interviewer: What are some practical ways a local assembly can fulfill the purpose of God? And in light of what you have said, *how* should a local assembly apply these practices?

Paul: There are five primary ways the Church, or more specifically any local assembly, fulfills its purpose in God. The first is *ministry*, which in a broad sense is the loving labors of the believers. The next is *evangelism*, which is the gathering together of the raw materials for God's house. The third is *discipleship*, which is the preparation of the individual materials. The fourth is *fellowship*, which is the fitting together of the materials into their respective places in the house. And the last is *praise*, which is the ongoing work of the completed house. As I expound upon each of these, I will establish both the *truth of their form* and the *spirit of their use.* Let me begin with ministry.

Interviewer: The word "ministry" has many meanings. What do you mean when you use the word?

Paul: I am speaking of believers serving other people in Jesus' name. In this sense, ministry pertains to the good works and loving labors of the believers. Jesus instructed His followers to let their *light so shine before men, that they may see your good works and glorify your Father in heaven* (Matthew 5:16). We build holy relationships and glorify God by doing good works before others in the name of Jesus. This is why I teach that whatever we do in word or deed, we must *do all in the name of the Lord Jesus* (Colossians 3:17).

Interviewer: What then is the *truth* about biblical ministry?

Paul: The *truth*, or we could say the form or structure, of biblical ministry is laid out in the Acts of the Apostles. For example, Luke wrote that the original Church met daily *in the temple, and breaking bread from house to house* (Acts 2:46). In other words, the original apostolic Church met for worship and ministry in both large congregational meetings and various private homes. The temple ministry provided an opportunity for mass teaching and evangelizing while the home ministry provided the kind of environment necessary for building strong and intimate relationships within the body. The relationship building that takes place in homes serves as a training ground for learning how to have a close, intimate relationship with God. These relationships form the foundation for the ministry, outreach, and growth of the Church.

Interviewer: So an essential part of the structure of the early Church were these home meetings.

Paul: Yes. Home meetings are fundamental. We owned no "church buildings" in those days, although that is not the reason we met in homes. The reason is because homes are part of the Lord's plan. Homes are where the "grass roots" shepherding of the Lord's people takes place.

Before the Lord came in the flesh, people went to the temple to worship God. But this approach to God was steeped in formalized ritual. Today, however, ever since the birth of the Messiah and especially since Pentecost, God dwells in a living temple...and the temple goes to people. Homes are where people live. The atmosphere is casual rather than formalistic, which is useful to Jesus in building the close personal relationships He desires to have with all believers and the close relationships between believers.

Interviewer: What about the leadership structure of a local assembly?

Paul: Well, here's what Luke wrote: *So when they had appointed elders in every church, and prayed with fasting, they commended them to the Lord in whom they had believed* (Acts 14:23). Local assemblies are led by groups of men called "elders" who are appointed by the founding apostolic team. These men may differ in giftings and ministries, but must be collegial in oversight authority.

Interviewer: What do you mean by *collegial*?

Paul: I mean that the authority vested in these colleagues is equally distributed. There is no "senior elder." All are equal in oversight authority.

Interviewer: Is there a specific advantage to this approach over, say, the single leader concept?

Paul: This *is* the single leader concept...only, the single leader is Jesus Christ, the Head of the Church. In addition, the collegial approach provides effective, up-close accountability among assembly overseers. It also provides continuity of oversight. For example, if one elder dies or falls into sin, the assembly continues under the oversight of the remaining elders. This plural oversight, the eldership, is always raising up additional elders to be added to the team. This is the biblical structure which over time preserves the Headship of Jesus Christ in the local assembly. The eldership serves as a transparent interface between the Head and the body, serving as a channel through which the Chief

Shepherd's oversight can flow out to His sheep.

Interviewer: So the benefit of this—would you call it a collegial eldership?—is the accountability and ministerial continuity it affords while preserving Jesus as the Head of His body. Is that right?

Paul: Yes. But don't overlook the spiritual benefits it has for the body of believers through the diverse gifts of the elders. I wrote of these God-given gifts to the church in Ephesus. *But to each one of us grace was given according to the measure of Christ's gift... And He Himself gave some to be apostles, some prophets, some evangelists, and some pastors and teachers, for the equipping of the saints for the work of ministry, for the edifying of the body of Christ...* (Ephesians 4:7, 11-12). All five of these "ascension gifts" operate and work together to equip the believers for ministry in the original Church. And ideally, all five ministries should be found in some dimension in every local eldership.

Interviewer: Could you provide us with a more detailed description of the work of these five ministries?

Paul: In a word, the work of apostles is initiation. They are the ones who gets things started, whether it's founding a church or establishing a doctrine. As an apostle, I see myself as an *architekton*, a "master builder." You see, just as an architect begins the process of building a house, an apostle begins the process of building a church. Once the assembly is firmly established, his work becomes that of preserving it on the solid foundation. But he hands the ongoing, day-to-day oversight over to a team of elders.

Interviewer: What about a prophet?

Paul: You must understand that there is a vast difference between someone used in the gift of prophecy and a prophet. Under the law of Moses, if a prophet's words failed to come to pass, he was to be put to death (Deuteronomy 18:20-22). Under the New Testament, his words are to be put to death; that is, they are to be disregarded. A man's prophetic gift must be proved over an extended period of time before he is recognized as a genuine prophet.

Once a man is so recognized, he should be regarded as a true spokesman of God. His primary work is to declare God's present word to the local assembly, or perhaps to the Church at large. He often works closely with an apostle in laying the foundation of a new assembly.

Interviewer: What about evangelists, pastors, and teachers?

Paul: Evangelists are preachers of the gospel. They are first and foremost soul-winners, specializing in bringing souls into the kingdom and teaching others to do likewise. Pastors guide and watch over the members of a local assembly. Their primary responsibilities involve discipling individual members and promoting unity among all the believers. Teachers work in conjunction with pastors in instructing members in the principles of God's Word. In many cases, pastors teach and teachers pastor.

Interviewer: These are all simple yet profound insights into the biblical structure of the body of Christ and its oversight under the Headship of Jesus. The Scriptures are very plain about the *truth* of ministry. Now what about the *spirit* of ministry? How can the Church minister most effectively to both itself and those outside the body?

Paul: Jesus described the spirit of ministry when He said to His disciples, *"You know that those who are considered rulers over the Gentiles lord it over them, and their great ones exercise authority over them. Yet it shall not be so among you; but whoever desires to become great among you shall be your servant. And whoever of you desires to be first shall be slave of all. For even the Son of Man did not come to be served, but to serve, and to give His life a ransom for many"* (Mark 10:42-45). This is the true spirit of ministry. Ministry is servanthood, not dictatorship. It is self-sacrifice, not self-exaltation.

This means that the true spirit of ministry invalidates all uses of coercion, intimidation, manipulation, or domination as instruments of leadership. Rather than devaluing their ministries by using these tactics to shepherd God's people, leaders must instead strive to always *speak the truth in love.* Truth without love is like having a tooth pulled without Novocain. It is harsh and painful and leads to the critical, condemning spirit of the Pharisees. On the other hand, love without truth leads to false doctrine, deception, and permissiveness. Jesus was full of both *grace and truth.* Together, these qualities form the foundation of His ministry in the Church and to the world.

Ultimately, the goal of spiritual ministry is to enable God's people through teaching and training to hear and obey the voice of God. Leaders are not charged with giving people answers for all their various and sundry problems; they are there to remove all hindrances so the people can hear from God for themselves. They are there to serve as a pattern and example for the people. I am not speaking against strong oversight, which may from time to time include forceful rebuke and firm correction; I am simply describing the spirit and purpose of it.

Interviewer: Your explanation of biblical ministry founded on grace and truth encompasses so much it hardly seems possible that there is more. But you said that there are five ways in which the Church can fulfill its purpose of glorifying God. What is the second way the body of Christ can glorify God in the earth?

Paul: The second way the Church fulfills its purpose is through *evangelism*, which is the work of seeking and saving those who are lost. Evangelism can be thought of as the gathering together of the building materials for the habitation of God. Jesus said, *"By this My Father is glorified, that you bear much fruit"* (John 15:8). We build holy relationships and glorify God by winning many souls to Jesus Christ, that He might be glorified in an innumerable company of believers. As local assemblies evangelize the lost, they glorify God and enlarge His eternal dwelling place.

Interviewer: Yes. The Scriptures say, *For it was fitting for Him, for whom are all things and by whom are all things, in bringing many sons to glory, to make the captain of their salvation perfect through sufferings* (Hebrews 2:10). It is clear that the Church glorifies God by seeking and saving the lost. But how do the sufferings of the Captain of our salvation relate to the Church evangelizing the lost?

Paul: The sufferings of Jesus first relate to the *truth*, or structure, of biblical evangelism. The heartbeat of the gospel concerns the sufferings of Jesus: His death for our sins, His burial, and His glorious resurrection on the third day—three elements that work together to bring salvation to a dying world. Praise be to God! We must preach no other gospel. And for any who do, let them be accursed! (Galatians 1:8).

Interviewer: I'm still not sure I understand how His sufferings establish a structure for evangelism.

Paul: His sufferings give structure to the way a person applies the gospel to his life so that he may be saved. The personal application of the gospel mirrors the sufferings of Christ, just as Luke presented in Acts 2:38. The death of Jesus is applied to a person when he repents of his sins (whereas Jesus died *for* sin, we must die *to* sin, Romans 6:2). His burial is applied through water baptism in the name of Jesus Christ (we are in fact "buried with Him in baptism," Romans 6:4a). And His resurrection is applied when a person receives the gift of the Holy Spirit (we rise from the waters of baptism to "walk in newness of life"—the Spirit-filled life, Romans 6:4b). The fact that the gospel must be obeyed in order to be believed and received is fundamental. Herein is the *truth* of evangelism.

Interviewer: Is the spirit of biblical evangelism the same as the spirit of biblical ministry?

Paul: Yes. Biblical evangelism requires the most fervent love and a deep serving spirit. It requires ministers to willingly lose all for the sake of Christ. It is this spirit that propelled me to write to the Corinthian Church, *I have become all things to all men, that I might by all means save some. Now this I do for the gospel's sake* (1 Corinthians 9:22-23). We must also be willing to give all for the saving of souls. As I also wrote, *And I will very gladly spend and be spent for your souls* (2 Corinthians 12:15). The sacrificial spirit of genuine love and holiness which emanates from the body of Christ gives credence to our message of salvation. We are the aroma of the knowledge of God to those who are being saved.

Interviewer: How exactly does biblical ministry differ from biblical evangelism? Isn't evangelism ministry?

Paul: Yes, but evangelism is ministering with the specific intention of winning the lost. The third way the Church can glorify God in the earth is ministry as well. But this ministry is specifically geared toward those who are already a part of the body of Christ. I'm referring to the ministry of **discipleship,** the preparing and perfecting of the saints. To continue the building analogy, discipleship can be thought of as the preparation of the individual materials that form the temple of the living God.

Discipleship pertains to the spiritual growth of the believers in personal holiness unto the Lord—the Word becoming flesh on an individual level. I taught the Corinthians this when I wrote, *Or do you not know that your body is the temple of the Holy Spirit who is in you, whom you have from God, and you are not your own? For you were bought at a price; therefore glorify God in your body and in your spirit, which are God's* (1 Corinthians 6:19-20). We build our relationship with God and glorify Him when we keep our bodies (our outward words, actions, and appearances) and our spirits (our inward thoughts, emotions, attitudes, motives, and desires) pure and holy in the sight of the Lord.

Interviewer: What then is the *truth* of biblical discipleship? How can a local church bring structure to this very important ministry?

Paul: Jesus said, *"A disciple is not above his teacher, but everyone who is perfectly trained will be like his teacher"* (Luke 6:40). The local assembly can *perfectly train* believers to become progressively more like Jesus through the laying of strong foundations. First the local assembly must be prepared to model Jesus before new believers, for as Jesus said, the new believers will become like their teachers. The assembly must also mentor new believers through one-on-one relationships, training them up in the ways of the Lord, much like parents train up their children. Such training must be gradual, the assembly feeding new believers the *pure milk of the Word* just as a mother feeds her newborn babe.

The assembly must be sensitive to when new believers are ready for the stronger meat of the Word. They must not feed them too much too soon, lest they choke the spiritual babes with too much truth. For those just weaned from the breasts, doctrine must be presented precept upon precept, line upon line, here a little, there a little.

Discipleship also involves ministering to the inner wounds that inhibit new believers from living for God. This is the ministry of *healing the brokenhearted*. Just as the believers were instructed to remove the graveclothes from Lazarus, believers today must free those whom Jesus has resurrected to life from the inner pain that keeps them in spiritual bondage. Jesus raises those who are dead in sin to newness of life, but the assembly must patiently persist in the hard work of freeing them from the trappings of their prior life.

Interviewer: How can a local assembly know when a believer no longer needs discipleship?

Paul: No longer needs discipleship? A believer will no longer need discipleship when He goes to be with the Lord. Until then, every believer needs discipleship, whether he has been a member of the body for five years or fifty years. Your question, however, leads directly to what I want to tell you about the *spirit* of biblical discipleship. Jesus said, *"So likewise, whoever of you does not forsake all that he has cannot be My disciple"* (Luke 14:33). The spirit of discipleship means making Jesus our highest priority. It is the forsaking of all—the counting of all things as loss that we might know Christ. Every believer is in the process of losing His life for Christ, some are just further along in the process than others. Discipleship, therefore, requires a spirit of patience and perseverance for both the disciple and those doing the discipling.

The truth about biblical discipleship, or shall I call it spiritual growth, is that it is ongoing. Today's believers should learn to focus on the journey itself, not just the end of the journey. The quality of the process determines the quality of the product. The finish line of spiritual growth is meeting the Lord in the air. Until then, we are all *pressing toward the goal,* in humble acknowledgment that none of us has yet *attained the prize.*

Interviewer: So because there is always room for growth, the *spirit* of biblical discipleship leaves no room for anyone to become haughty or proud.

Paul: Precisely. The love and humility required of biblical discipleship bonds together the newest babes with the most seasoned saints. Let me add, however, that for those called to a role in collegial eldership, the nature of the discipleship process changes. Because they have demonstrated a capacity for accurately discerning the Lord's voice, Jesus Himself is able to disciple them more directly. To qualify for this place of honor and responsibility, a man must have learned to live in consistent submission to God's authority and must have effectively crucified the passions and desires of the flesh (Galatians 5:24).

Interviewer: This sounds like a potentially dangerous situation. Couldn't it result in leaders dominating the assembly or going off on bizarre tangents?

Paul: It certainly could, which underscores the need for up-close, deliberate, and forceful accountability. Hence, a strong collegial eldership.

Interviewer: So the elders help keep each other in a right spirit before God—iron sharpening iron, so to speak.

Paul: Yes, along with whatever external apostolic and prophetic ministries are associated with the local assembly.

Interviewer: I see. But this means not pulling any

punches. Elders would have to be brutally honest with each other. I can see how participation in this kind of leadership structure would require exceedingly great humility and excellent character. How can a person know when he is ready for this?

Paul: Ministerial gifts must have become conspicuous in a person's life, gifts that are recognized by the elders and the majority of the local assembly. The person must have received sufficient training and equipping so that these gifts are adequately developed and tested. And there must be confidence that the person can accurately discern the voice of God.

Interviewer: This is all very interesting. While I think about what you have just said, please talk about the fourth way a local assembly fulfills its purpose.

Paul: The fourth way is *fellowship*. This can be thought of as the work of knitting together the building materials into a unified, harmonious body of believers. Fellowship enables the Word to become flesh on a corporate level, thereby glorifying God. Jesus said, *"And the glory which You gave Me I have given them, that they may be one just as We are one: I in them, and You in Me; that they may be made perfect in one, and that the world may know that You have sent Me, and have loved them as You have loved Me"* (John 17:22-23). We build relationships and glorify God by living and working together in unity. I wrote about this to the church in Rome saying, *Now may the God of patience and comfort grant you to be like-minded toward one another, according to Christ Jesus, that you may with one mind and one mouth glorify the God and Father of our Lord Jesus Christ* (Romans 15:5-6).

Interviewer: So the structure of fellowship is unity, right?

Paul: Yes! This is why I exhorted the Ephesians to *endeavor to keep the unity of the Spirit in the bond of peace* (Ephesians 4:3). Notice that I did not say unity of the body. This is because the body's unity is the result of God's people uniting with the Spirit of Jesus. If every one were united with the Spirit, the body would automatically be in unity. And for this to happen, the people of God must be humble and they must be fed sound doctrine, taught with authority and love.

Many don't seem to understand that doctrine is the foundation of unity. It is only by the study of correct doctrine that we can all eventually come together in a unity of faith. Doctrine, after all, defines what we believe. It's not enough to simply say you believe in Jesus. Who is Jesus? Who do the Scriptures identify Him as? During the days of the original church, every time false apostles came along preaching another Jesus, or another Spirit, or another gospel, the result was disunity. So keeping the unity of the Spirit requires more than a willingness to forebear and forgive; it ultimately requires a knowledge of sound doctrine.

As the believers become more knowledgeable of biblical doctrine, they will be better equipped to develop proper personal boundaries. These boundaries form the basis for all spiritual relationships between members of the body. They protect God's people by keeping them safe in the power of God. Establishing godly boundaries in the lives of believers is equivalent to the perfecting of personal holiness. In fact, boundaries is actually just another word for holiness.

Interviewer: You've introduced a new concept to me, Paul. Not necessarily about fellowship, but about *boundaries.* How can establishing boundaries between believers draw them closer together in biblical fellowship? It seems as though boundaries are meant to separate and isolate people, not connect them.

Paul: We all have boundaries, even if we don't acknowledge them. The problem is that some boundaries are biblical and some are not. Biblical boundaries are established for protection, not isolation. Solomon wrote, *Whoever has no rule over his own spirit is like a city broken down, without walls* (Proverbs 25:28). A city without walls is unprotected and will eventually be defeated. Jesus wants His body to be both protected and victorious, which is why He has established certain boundaries for His people.

You are right when you say that boundaries separate. But the purpose of this separation is better connections. In other words, the purpose of boundaries is love. What boundaries do is help us to understand where we stop and our brother begins—what we are responsible for and what our brother is responsible for. Strong and truly intimate relationships can only be formed when people are clear as to who they are and what they are responsible for in the relationship.

One of the common problems of boundary development concerns the believer's choice of building materials. When a believer constructs boundaries made of defensiveness, judgmentalism, bitterness, selfishness, or fear, he has built a wall of false security around his heart. I call these walls *strongholds*. These kinds of boundaries produce separation without connection. And like the walls around Jericho, these *imaginations* and *high things* must be cast down.

The goal of every believer must be to make Jesus his only stronghold. Solomon said, *The name of the LORD is a strong tower; the righteous run to it and are safe* (Proverbs 18:10). All ungodly strongholds must be torn down. Jesus must become our all—the only One we're depending on. This will be the ultimate outcome of all true spiritual healing and growth. As Jesus becomes our stronghold, we will no longer be separated by sin. Instead we will come to the *unity of the faith, growing up into Jesus in all things, unto a perfect man, unto the stature of the fulness of Christ* (Ephesians 4:13). This is genuine unity in Jesus Christ.

Interviewer: Well, I understand that a believer must tear down all strongholds that rise up against the knowledge of God. You made that clear in your second letter to the Corinthians. But what are the practical ways that believers can make Jesus their stronghold? Right now it all sounds rather theoretical.

Paul: The practical ways we make Jesus our only stronghold begin in the home, among our closest relations. As the basic relational unit of the body of Christ, God has established some clear and specific boundaries between family members. For example, wives are to *submit to their own husbands, as to the Lord. For the husband is head of the wife, as also Christ is head of the church; and He is the Savior of the body* (Ephesians 5:22-23). In addition, children are to *obey their parents in all things, for this is well pleasing to the Lord.* And fathers are not to *provoke their children, lest they become* *discouraged* (Colossians 3:20-21).

These boundaries point to the need for family relationships based on biblical principles of authority and submission, and truth and grace. When believers embrace these principles, they effectively make Jesus their stronghold. The Scriptures are replete with practical teachings on boundaries, including how employers and employees are to relate, how members of the body of Christ are to relate, and how each of us is to relate to God. Biblical boundaries bring structure to relationships giving them great and enduring strength.

Interviewer: What you are really saying, then, is that boundaries are the *truth* of biblical fellowship.

Paul: Yes, and the spirit of biblical fellowship is humility, kindness, and mutual concern for others. I taught all the churches to hold fast to the spirit of biblical fellowship when I wrote exhortations such as: *Submitting to one another in the fear of God* (Ephesians 5:21); *In lowliness of mind let each esteem others better than himself. Let each of you look out not only for his own interests, but also for the interests of others* (Philippians 2:3-4); *Rejoice with those who rejoice, and weep with those who weep... as much as depends on you, live peaceably with all men* (Romans 12:15, 18); *We then who are strong ought to bear with the scruples of the weak, and not to please ourselves* (Romans 15:1). When the body of believers have this spirit working in their hearts, they will be *knit together in love* producing true biblical fellowship.

Interviewer: Ministry, evangelism, discipleship, fellowship. The truths you have brought out about each one of these sets the body of Christ apart from the world. I don't think I'm being too grandiose when I say that there is no comparison between the Church of the Living God and any other organization of people that has existed in the history of the world.

Paul: The Church of the living God is not an organization, it is a living organism, a body. The Church is a holy assembly serving a holy God. The body of Christ stands on the firm foundation of God's truth and operates through the power of His Spirit. This alone makes His bride separate and distinct from the organizations of the world. But what further sets the Church apart is that it reverently and fervently acknowledges Jesus as the one and only true and living God. This is the fifth way the Church glorifies God in the earth—*praise*, the joyful, heart-felt expressions of adoration and appreciation offered by the redeemed believers to the Giver of Eternal Life. This is the overarching work of God's dwelling place as it is being constructed and perfected.

Interviewer: And if there was anyone who knew how to praise God, it was the man after God's own heart.

Paul: Yes. David wrote, *I will praise You, O LORD, with my whole heart; I will tell of all Your marvelous works* (Psalms 9:1); *Whoever offers praise glorifies Me; and to him who orders his conduct aright I will show the salvation of God* (Psalms 50:23); *Let everything that has breath praise the LORD. Praise the LORD!* (Psalms 150:6). We glorify God by praising Him and thanking Him from the depths of our hearts. If everyone on earth would praise the Lord, His glory would fill the earth as the waters cover the sea, in fulfillment of the purpose of God!

Interviewer: Then the *truth* about biblical praise would have to do with the various ways in which we praise the Lord.

Paul: You are really catching on to this. According to the Scriptures, we are to praise God by shouting, clapping, dancing, singing, raising our hands, rejoicing, and playing musical instruments. As you can see, there is nothing quiet or reserved about the way God desires His Church to praise Him.

Interviewer: Of course! Why would we praise God quietly if the whole purpose of praise is to make Him known?

Paul: Precisely. But the *spirit* in which we magnify the Lord is also crucial. When we praise God, it must come from an adoring, appreciative heart. Praise is intended to be a freewill offering to God. This precludes any kind of manipulation, coercion, or intimidation from the leader of a praise service. The bride must willingly express her love for the Husband, otherwise her expressions are meaningless.

Interviewer: So you're saying that if it's coerced or manipulated in any way, it ceases to be genuine praise.

Paul: Yes. It may please the praise leader, but won't please God. Jesus never coerced anyone to praise Him. He didn't want anyone to appease Him as a man; He wanted them to willingly praise Him as God.

Interviewer: You have talked about five areas of ministry through which the members of a local church can glorify God. I was thinking that there are also five ascension gifts that Jesus has given to the Church. Is there any relationship between the five gifts and the five areas of ministry?

Paul: Yes. Even though everyone involved in the oversight of a congregation can and should be involved in all five areas to some degree and there is often much overlapping; nevertheless, each ascension gift has something unique to contribute to a particular area. For example, apostolic gifts relate directly to ministry: establishing the pattern, modeling the spirit, setting the course, guiding the way. Evangelists are obviously involved directly in evangelism, while teachers are involved in discipleship, and pastors, who are concerned for the welfare of the flock at large, are involved in fellowship. Those with prophetic gifts tend to be most directly involved in praise.

When a church receives ministry from all five gifts on a regular basis, even if some of the ministry comes from outside the local assembly, the spiritual health of the church will be maximized. And a healthy church is a growing church.

End-time Power and Glory

Interviewer: You've enabled us to look back to the past by presenting us with a marvelous sketch of the first century Church. This helps us to envision far more accurately the glorious Church that Jesus will present to Himself. It also helps us to know how Jesus expects us to work with Him in building that Church in our local assemblies. What can you now tell us about the immediate future?

Paul: Let me confine my remarks to some specific areas that pertain directly to the preparation of the glorious Church. It is clear that the Church is living in perilous times. Persecution of Christians is on the increase and trouble is arising on every side. Abortion-on-demand, homosexual marriages, legalized casino gambling, widespread immorality, the systematic assault on faith by public education, wanton violence, and ceaseless war all point to the proliferation of the antichrist spirit in the world.

Daniel spoke of these times when he wrote: *And there shall be a time of trouble, such as never was since there was a nation, even to that time. And at that time your people shall be delivered, every one who is found written in the book. And many of those who sleep in the dust of the earth shall awake, some to everlasting life, some to shame and everlasting contempt. Those who are wise shall shine like the brightness of the firmament, and those who turn many to righteousness like the stars forever and ever* (Daniel 12:1-3).

Interviewer: Are you saying that widespread persecution will soon come upon the Church?

Paul: Yes, persecution is a principle: *All who desire to live godly in Christ Jesus will suffer persecution* (2 Timothy 3:12). This is not to say that everyone will experience the same intensity of persecution. But to deny there will be widespread persecution is to deny the principles of the Scriptures.

Interviewer: What do you mean?

Paul: I mean that persecution is a prerequisite to power and glory. If the Church is to have great power and glory, she must be willing to face severe persecution. Peter summarized this principle when he wrote, *But rejoice to the extent that you partake of Christ's sufferings, that when His glory is revealed, you may also be glad with exceeding joy. If you are reproached for the name of Christ, blessed are you, for the Spirit of glory and of God rests upon you* (1 Peter 4:13-14).

Many people are concerned about the need for a greater anointing upon the Church, but this cannot come apart from persecution. Don't forget, it was at the time when great persecution arose against the church at Jerusalem that Philip went to Samaria and worked great miracles. Just as the power of resurrection can only come after suffering and death, so the demonstration of great power and glory can only come after great suffering and persecution. This is an unchanging, inviolable principle.

Interviewer: Are you predicting a steady increase in persecution against the Church?

Paul: Yes, at least for those in the Church who are intensely interested in advancing the kingdom of God and seeing His glory.

Interviewer: What else do you see lying ahead?

Paul: In His parable of the wheat and the tares, Jesus said, *"At the time of harvest I will say to the reapers, 'First gather together the tares and bind them in bundles to burn them, but gather the wheat into my barn.'"* (Matthew 13:30). This passage indicates that at some point prior to His return, the tares, representing false brethren, will be separated from the glorious Church and gathered together into a false church. This sovereign act of God will remove from the Church all things that hinder her from becoming the glorious Church, without spot or wrinkle. At that time she will become a Church of great power and glory.

Interviewer: A Church of great power and glory! The purpose of God fulfilled!

Paul: Not yet. John wrote, *Then I heard a loud voice saying in heaven, "Now salvation, and strength, and the kingdom of our God, and the power of His Christ have come."* When will this great power come? When the *"accuser of our brethren, who accused them before our God day and night, has been cast down"* (Revelation 12:10). Moreover, Isaiah wrote that God *will destroy on this mountain the surface of the covering cast over all people, and the veil that is spread over all nations* (Isaiah 25:7). Once Satan and his host have been cast out of the heavens and confined to the earthly realm, the veil of demonic principalities and powers that presently shrouds the earth will be removed and the Church will be liberated from these spiritual obstructions. At that time her oneness with her Head will be perfected.

Interviewer: But Satan will be on earth?

Paul: Yes. If the Church really wants great power and glory, she will have to trade her creature comforts for it. You see, once Satan is confined to the earthly realm, he will no longer be able to operate in the spiritual realm. This means that the only way he will be able to continue his war against the Church will be by inhabiting a human host. We can presently observe a vast army of mind-numbed, media-warped adolescents standing willing and eager to host the hordes of demonic spirits soon to descend upon the earth. These spirit-empowered minions will have one purpose: to wreak havoc on the Church of the living God.

John wrote that *it was granted to him to make war with the saints and to overcome them* (Revelation 13:7). During this time, the Church will be overcome in the flesh, just as Jesus was overcome in the flesh through the crucifixion. But simultaneously the Church will be victorious in the spirit.

John described the Church's ultimate victory when he wrote: *And they overcame him by the blood of the Lamb and by the word of their testimony, and they did not love their lives to the death* (Revelation 12:11). Jesus told His disciples about this time when He said, *"Then they will deliver you up to tribulation and kill you, and you will be hated by all nations for My name's sake...But he who endures to the end shall be saved. And this gospel of the kingdom will be preached in all the world as a witness to all the nations, and then the end will come"* (Matthew 24:9, 13-14).

You see, when the Church is comfortable, she loses her spiritual intensity. This is why the prophet warns, *"Woe to you who are at ease in Zion"* (Amos 6:1). But when Satan unleashes the raw power of evil in a worldwide host of godless, persecuting storm-troopers, the Church will suddenly be transformed from a Church at ease to a Church in action. Then the gospel will be preached in all the world with mighty and irrefutable power.

Interviewer: Ever since her reestablishment as a nation in 1948, the eyes of many Christians have been on the tiny nation of Israel. How will the persecution you have described impact your Jewish brethren?

Paul: I can tell you this, I have *continual sorrow and grief in my heart* for those among my people who have rejected the Hope of Israel (Romans 9:2). But I am also very concerned about those Gentile believers who have failed to appreciate the place Israel holds in the heart of God.

Let me simply say this: Up to this point in time, most of the natural branches have been broken off of the Church and many branches wild by nature have been grafted in. But as I warned the Gentiles in Rome, these wild branches would be wise to consider that *if God did not spare the natural branches, He may not spare them either* (Romans 11:21).

Yes, it's true that blindness has happened to Israel, but only in part and only *until the fulness of the Gentiles has come in. And so all Israel will be saved* (Romans 11:25-26). Israel is key to the fulfillment of God's end-time promises. Those who ignore this reality or downplay its significance do so at their own peril.

Interviewer: And the significance of the persecution?

Paul: The persecution will purify the motives of the Church, which will result in a deep and profound burden for the Jews of Israel. Remember, the gospel must be preached in every nation, and that includes the nation of Israel, where it will ultimately have it's greatest effect.

Interviewer: And what will happen once the Jews of Israel come into the Church?

Paul: *If their being cast away is the reconciling of the world, what will their acceptance be but life from the dead?* (Romans 11:15). Once the Jews of Israel are grafted into the body of Christ through the Acts 2:38 plan of salvation, the dead will rise and we who are alive and remain will be caught up together with them to meet the Lord in the air!

The Will of God

Interviewer: It sounds as though the last days will be full of excitement and high drama, but it also sounds rather scary. How will the Church, both Jews and Gentiles, make it through such intense persecution? How will anyone "endure to the end"?

Paul: Jesus has a very simple plan for enduring to the end: It's called, *Do the will of God.* John admonished that *the world is passing away, and the lust of it; but he who does the will of God abides forever.* He then revealed that *it is the last hour; and as you have heard that the Antichrist is* *coming, even now many antichrists have come, by which we know that it is the last hour* (1 John 2:17-18).

For the Church to endure severe persecution en mass without experiencing a wholesale capitulation to the forces of evil, she must be sustained by an ever-flowing supply of the power of God. Peter wrote that we are *kept by the power of God through faith for salvation ready to be revealed in the last time. In this you greatly rejoice, though now for a little while, if need be, you have been grieved by various trials, that the genuineness of your faith, being much more precious than gold that perishes, though it is tested by fire, may be found to praise, honor, and glory at the revelation of Jesus Christ...* (1 Peter 1:5-7).

Interviewer: How do we access this power? What can we do to insure that we are continually infused with it?

Paul: The answer is clear: We must line up fully with the purpose of God. No degree of compromise is acceptable to God.

Interviewer: But when will the end come? When will the purpose of God be fulfilled?

Paul: God's purpose will be fulfilled when the biblically structured Church preaches the true gospel throughout *all the world as a witness to all the nations.* Only then will the end come. Only then will the glory of the Lord fill the earth as the waters cover the sea.

Interviewer: I know we are to walk by faith and not by sight, but everything you are saying seems so remote and extraordinary.

Paul: In the words of Isaiah, *The LORD of hosts has sworn, saying, "Surely, as I have thought, so it shall come to pass, and as I have purposed, so it shall stand."* (Isaiah 14:24). Whatever the Lord has purposed to do, He will do. We can count on that. He is well able to accomplish whatever He determines He wants to accomplish. *The purpose of God is unstoppable!* This means that God *will* fill the earth with the knowledge of His glory. He *will* live in intimate fellowship with redeemed man for eternity.

Interviewer: I believe that God is able to accomplish His purpose. But if His purpose is to live in intimate fellowship with redeemed man for eternity, why aren't all men redeemed? If it is His purpose that every person be saved, why hasn't that happened?

Paul: You are confusing the will of God with the purpose of God. There is a significant difference between the two. While the *purpose* of God is dependent upon the choice of *God*, the *will* of God is dependent upon the choice of *man*. This is why Jesus taught His disciples to pray, "Your will be done on earth as it is in heaven" (Matthew 6:10). The will of God is what God *desires* to take place, while the purpose of God is what He has *determined* will take place.

In answering your question, you must understand that it is *good and acceptable in the sight of God our Savior, who desires all men to be saved and to come to the knowledge of the truth* (1 Timothy 2:3-4). It is the *will of God* that everyone be saved, but we also know that not everyone will be saved. God's *purpose* is to save only those who believe His Word. And not everything that happens is the will of God. But in spite of this fact, God is able to take whatever happens and cause it to work toward the furtherance of His purpose. In fact, *we know that all things work together for good to those who love God, to those who are the called according to His purpose* (Romans 8:28).

Interviewer: Then it is man's responsibility to see the will of God come to pass.

Paul: Yes. This is why I admonished the Ephesians not to be *unwise, but understand what the will of the Lord is* (Ephesians 5:17). Each one of us is personally responsible for doing the will of God, whatever it may be.

Interviewer: I feel like I'm echoing the question of Acts 2:37 when I ask this, but Paul, what must we do to be actively committed to the purpose of God? What must we do to be saved?

Paul: We must be about the business of aligning our local assemblies with every biblical structure and principle. We must become open and vulnerable to one another as brethren. We must forego all hidden agendas and self-serving initiatives. As Solomon wrote, *Many are the plans in a man's heart, but it is the Lord's purpose that prevails* (Proverbs 19:21, NIV).

As perilous times come upon us, it is vital that we all become committed, purely and simply, to the purpose of God. I can assure you that every minister of the gospel with a hidden agenda will be snared by that agenda. Jesus has given us a pattern to follow, and as we follow His pattern, doing exactly what He directs us to do, we can rest assured that God will build His dwelling place, both in great numbers and in spectacular spiritual strength. As only the Head is able to do, He will cause His body to increase with the increase that is from God.

To God our Savior, Who alone is wise,
be glory and majesty,
dominion and power,
both now and forever. Amen.
Jude 25

A final word from the authors...

The purpose of this book is to plant seeds. It is to provoke apostolic men and women to stop and consider: Are we currently headed in the right direction, or do we need to make some radical changes to line up with God's plan for the Church? We have attempted to describe the Church Jesus Christ is building as it appears in the Scriptures. Understanding and receiving the elements of this description is vital if the body of Christ is to stand victorious against the growing persecution, glorifying Jesus throughout the earth. God's people must be prepared, and that preparation must begin now. We ask that you please consider the points we have presented and pray with us that Jesus would lead each of us into "all truth" by the power of His glorious Spirit. Amen.

David Huston and Jim McKinley

If you are interested in more details on the major themes discussed in this book, please take a look at our web site. The address is...

www.gloriouschurch.com

If you would like to contact us for any reason, you may call or write to:

David Huston and Jim McKinley
PO Box 337, Carlisle, PA 17013
(717) 249-2059
DAHuston@aol.com
Leaders@gulftel.com

Other material from ...

Rosh Pinnah
P U B L I C A T I O N S

→

The Tip of the Arrow in Apostolic Publishing

● Solid content
● Practical tools for ministry
● Inspirational books for believers

Acts 29...Continuing the Apostolic Revival Through Spiritual Leadership Training by Theodore D. Grosbach

Laboring with the Lord, Missionary Ted Grosbach has been instrumental in establishing a strong and growing church in the nation of Zambia. He has accomplished this largely by training and releasing many men and women into leadership roles and through home fellowship groups, organized and supervised at the local church level. The combination of well-equipped leadership and home groups has propelled the Zambian church into ongoing, book-of-Acts style revival. Bro. Grosbach has now recorded the principles of leadership he teaches. These principles are worth studying and implementing, not because they work (and they do), but because they are biblical. Paperback, 14.95; 2 or more copies $14.00; 6 or more copies $10.50 each.

The Sons of Oil by David A. Huston

Find out how you can escape the hurts of the past so you can live for Jesus with all your heart in the present. Plus, learn how you can minister inner healing to other hurting people. Paperback, $8.95; 2 or more copies $8.00 each; 6 or more copies $5.50 each.

"The Sons of Oil is a wonderful book...a great book."
■ Jeff Arnold, Gainesville, FL

The Sons of Oil (book-on-tape)

This unabridged audio version brings to life the concepts described in the book. Dramatic readers create a book-on-tape that is both profound and enjoyable. A great gift for ministers or those who are hurting. Three-tape set, $10.95; 2 or more sets $10.00 each; 6 or more sets $7.50 each.

Powerful Effects ◆ Powerful Choices by Michelle Dangiuro

Full of facts and testimonies, this book gets to the root of "television addiction" and arms parents and pastors with the knowledge to combat TV's influence on the family and the Church. Paperback, $8.95; 2 or more copies $8.00 each; 6 or more copies $5.50 each.

Evidence of Things Not Seen by David A. Huston

Discover the principles that lie at the heart of our Apostolic Faith and learn how they must be expressed in our lives...to the glory of God! Paperback, $6.95; 2 or more copies $6.00 each; 6 or more copies $4.50 each.

The Real Message of John 3:16 by David A. Huston

Did you know that the Oneness of God and baptism in Jesus' name can be found in John 3:16? This eye-opening book plumbs the depths of the original text to refute the doctrine of the trinity and the modern theory of "easy-believism." Paperback, $6.95; 2 or more copies $6.00 each; 6 or more copies $4.50 each.

Healing Hands by David A. Huston

Is it always God's will to heal His people? Absolutely! Some may question this answer, but this faith-building book will prove it to be correct. It will also provoke you to examine your own spiritual life under the penetrating light of God's Word. Paperback, $4.95; 2 or more copies $4.50 each; 6 or more copies $3.50 each.

Building a Tabernacle of Prayer by David A. Huston

A practical guide to learning how to pray in the Presence of God. Booklet plus 90-minute cassette tape, $4.95; additional booklets $1.95 each.

☆

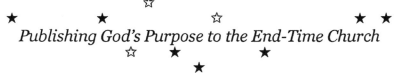

★   ★   ☆   ★ ★

Publishing God's Purpose to the End-Time Church

☆   ★   ★

★

Place orders by writing or calling...

Rosh Pinnah Publications

PO Box 337, Carlisle, PA 17013
(717) 258-5984 or (717) 249-2059
RoshPinnah@aol.com

Please add 10% to all orders for shipping.

Learning to Speak

Kingdom Language

Death and life are in the power of the tongue (Proverbs 18:21).

"But I say to you that for every idle word men may speak, they will give account of it in the day of judgment. For by your words you will be justified, and by your words you will be condemned" (Matthew 12:36-37).

More than anything else, our words demonstrate which kingdom we are part of: the kingdom of God or the kingdom of the devil. The words of the kingdom of God are spiritual. They are marked by grace and truth. They lift up and build up other people. The words of the devil tend to be deceptive, unkind, controlling, or destructive. Let's help one another learn to use "kingdom language."

Kingdom Language	Verse	Devil Language
Truthful, honest words	Ephesians 4:25	Lying, dishonest words
Edifying words (words designed to strengthen)	Ephesians 4:29	Corrupt words (words designed to subvert or ruin)
Kind, tender, forgiving words (words designed to heal)	Ephesians 4:31-32	Bitter, angry, malicious words (words designed to harm)
Thankful, appreciative words	Ephesians 5:4	Filthy, foolish words (profanity; crude, off-color jokes)
Spiritual singing	Ephesians 5:6-7,18-19	Hollow, deceptive words
Open and honest confession of faults	James 4:11, 5:16	Critical, condemning, accusing words
Prayerful words	James 4:16, 5:16	Boastful, arrogant, self-willed words
Controlled, deliberate words	Proverbs 10:19	Excessive, impulsive words
Wise words intended to dispense godly knowledge	Proverbs 15:7, 18:6	Contentious, competitive words intended to win an argument
Righteous, unperverted words	Proverbs 8:8, 20:19	Gossip and flattering words
Words that honor God and other people	Proverbs 27:2	Self-praising, self-exalting words
		Sarcasm (indirect hostility) Threats (direct hostility) Complaining (hostility toward God) Conversation that dominates the other person (non-stop talking)

He who guards his mouth preserves his life, but he who opens wide his lips shall have destruction (Proverbs 13:3).

"I have purposed that my mouth shall not transgress" (Psalms 17:3).

"Let the words of my mouth and the meditation of my heart be acceptable in Your sight, O LORD, my strength and my Redeemer" (Psalms 19:14).

<u>Agreement of Participants</u>

I agree that any participant may interrupt me at any time to call to my attention that I am not speaking kingdom language (or to warn me that I may not be speaking kingdom language).

When this happens...

> I will stop talking immediately to consider the nature of my words.

> I will not question the person or challenge their assertion in any way.

> I will use this information about myself to help me keep my words within the boundary of God's kingdom.

I also agree not to tell any other participant that he or she is not speaking kingdom language unless I really believe it to be true and really want to help the person. In other words, I will not do it as a gag or because I don't want to hear what's being said.

I understand that this is not a game. Everyone who participates should take it seriously. If we will all be judged by our words, then we need to help each other use the right kinds of words.

How forceful are right words!
Job 6:25

And whatever you do in word or deed, do all
in the name of the Lord Jesus,
giving thanks to God the Father through Him.
Colossians 3:17